I hate this book!

Harrison John

Radioactive Luminous Paint – a cardinal derailment of watchmaking

A sarcastic contribution to a sad story – should we laugh or should we cry?

Bibliographic information published by the
Deutsche Nationalbibliothek:

The Deutsche Nationalbibliothek lists this publication in the
Deutsche Nationalbibliografie; detailed bibliographic data
are available on the Internet at http://dnb.dnb.de

© 2023, Harrison John
Production and published by:
BoD - Books on Demand, Norderstedt

July 2023

ISBN: 9783755716839

**Danger
Radioactive
substance**

'Oh, I've discovered something wonderful, I can make my watch glow and read the time in the dark if I only knew what all the numbers mean', said Little Joe Hickerberg, son of Bernie Hickerberg.

Joe's father, Bernie Hickerberg, had married his younger sister Emma after his Dad ran off with Ava, Bernie's first wife and half-sister, a child of his mother and her grandfather. Dad and Ava were both declared dead, not because Bernie held a grudge, but to collect the $1.500 from Dad's life insurance policy.

Bernie Hickerberg and his sister Emma had seven children together, adding up to thirteen in the house, counting the five left with Bernie from his marriage to his first half-sister Ava and an illegitimate child living with them – said Little Joe – Bernie had fathered along the way with his eldest sister Olivia.

Whatever, child support had been claimed for only nine of them, because thirteen is already so far into double figures, that they couldn't do the math.

Little Joe's discovery became a tremendous success in the watch industry and came in very handy for this 'homogeneous' family in making ends meet, besides growing corn with an uneven number of rows, a phenomenon similar to strange deviations in human mental development. The Hickerbergs got it made ...

Normally, corn always has an even number of rows on each spikelet. The number of rows is always even because the spikelets appear in pairs and each spikelet produces two flowers: a fertile flower and a sterile flower. So, nature usually provides an even number of rows or lines. A watermelon, for example, has an even number of stripes. 'Special circumstances' in an unnatural environment could theoretically result in a spikelet with an odd number of rows. However, looking through a microscope, you'll probably find an invisible row that's just not fully developed. Imagine a cell dividing. That would be two, and if it continues like this, regularly and according to the norms, the result will always be an even number.

Well, this is how our sad story could begin and the origination of the idea of putting radioactive luminous paint on civilian watches would be better understandable ...

... but to tell the truth, it wasn't the idea of Little Joe Hickerberg. 'Real' scientists with a pedigree like you and me, and large parts of the watch industry in general, have been responsible for this terrible nonsense.

The first commercially viable luminous paint activated by radium (radium-226) was developed in the early 20th century by 'Geheimrat' (privy councilor) Arthur Junghans together with Marie Skłodowska Curie, better known as Mme Curie, the famous two-time Nobel Prize winner and 'discoveress' of the radium. It was applied to watches made by Junghans, once the world's largest producer of watches and clocks. Others soon followed with their own 'mixture' and opinions are divided as to who was actually the first.

Given the state of knowledge about radioactivity at the time, we shouldn't throw too much dirt on the early protagonists, and can only quote – slightly modified:

'For they did not know – yet – what they do.'

The strongest criticism, however, must be directed primarily to the ones who have followed later and created a worldwide demand for this irresponsible idiocy.

In the early beginnings, this was an extremely interesting innovation for the military, especially around the two World Wars.

For obvious reasons, it was better to read the time without an external light source, in an airplane or the trenches. But in the civilian world, this was an utterly stupid thing to do.

But what the military has, a 'man' must also have, and the nonsense continued at a rapid pace – in the civilian watch industry, polluting the world with radioactive material, often far beyond the end of our days.

True, Radium and radioactivity were for a long time considered harmless, even beneficial to health, and extraordinary healing powers were attributed to this new discovery.

Today's nuclear medicine does a highly beneficial job when radioactivity is used sensibly, purposefully, and in the right doses, and ionizing radiation isn't used unworldly and negligently in a way that – in retrospect and according to today's state of knowledge – must be considered completely insane.

Watches, time, and the universe

Watches, mechanical or more modern, are among the most fascinating objects ever devised by man. Their contribution to progress isn't only something we should call valuable – it was essential. I wouldn't say that we would still eat raw meat without the invention of watches and clocks, but we would certainly not stand where we are today. It would lead too far to list all the mechanic-, electric-, electronic-, tuning fork regulated- or quartz-controlled watches which have been produced until today – up to the atomic clock.

I also want to skip going into detail about the first precise and reliable <u>portable</u> timepieces which made it possible to better determine longitude at sea and thus greatly changed the world. Ships could now sail along shorter and safer routes, giving seafaring an enormous boost and driving pirates and other maritime riffraff of the time into bankruptcy and their descendants to Wall Street. They could no longer lurk for booty anywhere along the standard routes that had previously been more or less compulsory. As we know from the documentary 'Mutiny on the Bounty', one of these watches was stolen by Marlon Brando.

These more individual and shorter routes also drastically reduced the incidence of diseases typical of long sea voyages, such as scurvy.

All of this will be familiar to watch and clock aficionados – these were the high points, not the low points, of the business.

From the discoveries of the physical laws of the pendulum and the phenomenon of isochronism by Galileo Galilei and their application in watchmaking, up to a freely oscillating balance wheel and later a regulation by a quartz crystal, we've moved up from 1 Hertz (oscillation/s per second) to 32,768 Hertz (ultra-high quartz watches go even up to 262,144 Hertz).

The 'atomic-clocks' 'tick' at a stunning frequency of 9,192,631,770 Hertz, and via radio transmission, they can also frequently correct the accuracy of our watches on the wrist.

The maximum time deviations went down considerably to +/- 1 second in several million years. In short-term operation, the target of a maximum deviation of +/- 1 second in one billion years has already been reached.

'Simply' put: One second in an atomic clock is the duration of 9,192,631,770 periods of radiation corresponding to the transition between two hyperfine levels of the ground state of the Cesium 133 atom, set to rest at a temperature of 0 degrees Kelvin.

Exact time is not only useful when trying to catch a bus. Precise time measurements are also necessary to calculate speed, distance, and position, e.g. when we think about the GPS system. Therefore, the satellites orbiting above us have their own (or several) atomic clocks on board, sacrificing a little precision for weight and size, achieving an accuracy of +/- 1 second in 10,000 years.

Nevertheless, the first moon landings had already been successfully undertaken with highly precise mechanical watches on the wrists of the astronauts (and, of course, lots of other instruments inside the cabin).

Whether all of this has to be topped by even higher frequency 'quantum clocks' or 'optical clocks' or 'nuclear-optical clocks' or by the many ideas that have absolutely nothing to do with the accuracy of a watch, must be left to the ever-advancing modern watchmaking industry, although watches, especially those on the wrist, have become rather superfluous – not for the collectors and watch enthusiasts, of course.

We know since long that a complete rotation of the Earth around the sun lasts longer than 365 days (about 0.25 days more), so we must add a day to our calendar every 4 years.

The rotation of the Earth around its axis, representing 1 full day, isn't constant. It's even worse – it's slowing down overall, making our planet less than ideal as a master clock.

400 million years ago, a day had 22 hours according to our today's measuring standards because of the faster rotation of the Earth back then. To cope with this, and to keep the old records of Jesse Owens comparable, we leave the time standard as it is and squeeze in a 'leap second' now and then. This is not quite so easy, however, because the Earth's behavior varies in this respect.

The theory of the tides was formulated by Sir Isaac Newton many moons ago (in 1687 to be precise), and it's indeed the moon, that's responsible. Its gravitational pull causes ebb and flow and tidal friction that runs counter to the Earth's rotation. This slowing of the Earth's rotation, in turn, causes the Moon to move farther and farther away, three to four centimeters per year; Sir Newton was not aware of the latter, but you know it now – reading educates.

Tourists visiting the Royal Observatory in Greenwich will find a line set into the pavement – the Greenwich Meridian or Zero Meridian, dividing the globe into an Eastern and a Western hemisphere. If you then take out your smartphone with a satellite navigation app, you will quickly realize that it doesn't show 0 degrees. Only 102 meters further East, you will find the true Zero Meridian. What's gone wrong? Former explanations blaming a continental drift proved to be false. They simply made a mistake back in the 19th century, which has meanwhile been corrected – thanks to GPS and exact time.

One of the rules of the universe is 'angular momentum', which can do anything, slower, faster, sideways, while the total of the aggregate forces does not change. Mars and its moon Phobos have a different relationship than Earth and its moon – exactly the opposite is happening here. Mars is accelerated by Phobos, so the Martians are on a merry-go-round that spins faster and faster. At the same time, Phobos is spiraling inwards towards Mars. They will collide in about 50 million years, whilst our moon is moving away. Our Earth will remain at a complete standstill without a moon, but very long before the end it will be uninhabitable, and emigrating to Mars isn't an option.

Now brace yourself: Some of the radioactive dirt in the luminous paint on watches and clocks will still be there at this distant point in time when the last surviving insects have died out, leaving only a few resistant bacteria behind, which will subsequently also disappear in the remaining dust. No joke – especially the 'eternally radiating' Samarium 147!

'Don't carelessly play around with radioactivity, you horological nincompoops!'

As already mentioned: With some benevolence, we don't want to judge too harshly those responsible for this unwise behavior in the earlier days, but along with the ongoing progress of science, the following actors on the watchmaking stage should have 'seen the light' much earlier, clearly realizing what they were doing (wrong).

Gimmicks and derailments

Whenever a certain technological level was reached in watchmaking, sufficient for the time, but occasionally, even before that, 'creativity' went astray in all directions, and all too often into totally senseless areas.

With an accuracy of +/- 10 seconds per day, one can concentrate on all sorts of nonsense and let others find a higher precision, whereby the saying *'taste is always a matter of opinion'* has often been badly overused.

Movement 'decorations' (utterly useless engravings on the movement that drives the watch) are all the rage, even though the vast majority of people who wear a watch can't even open the back to look at it.

All too often, the dial of a watch has become the playground of artistic 'designers', and many a road accident has probably been the result of a vain attempt to read the time.

And then they realized that the gear train could be used not only to move the hands but also to 'mechanize' certain displays of 'adult entertainment' on the dial. Particularly popular: the copulating priest and nun.

17

Some 'complications' (as they are called in connection with watches and clocks) like a date display, a day display, or a month display, certainly have their value, while a moon phase will sooner or later be ignored and become a mere 'knickknack' – an indication that sooner or later deviates from reality and remains unadjusted, because the time it takes to set everything correctly soon becomes annoying.

An alarm function is nice; no objection here.

But then, the 'Divers'! – watches that are watertight up to a depth of 1000 meters, while their wearers will never submerge below a surface of a few feet. These timepieces are, admittedly, nicely shielded under the shower or well protected against humidity in general.

If you wear them on your wrist in the public swimming pool, they can't be stolen by thieves in the locker room (but occasionally they have to be fished out of the filter basket).

We also see special 'divers'-watches with a helium valve (no, that's no joke!). When sitting in a decompression chamber after a dive, this valve can be used to release helium from inside the case before the crystal is blown off.

During 'saturation diving', the ultra-fine molecules of the helium gas (pumped into the diving bell to improve the breathing gas) can penetrate the watch. But: With such a thing on the wrist of a professional diver, who wants to go down with it, they would have to immediately check his 'smoking habits' or see if the bottle of schnapps is empty again.

He, who wants to participate in a tourist scuba diving course with such a 'diver' watch, would immediately be sorted out. Poor readability and, all too often, the life-threatening possibility of moving the bezel in either direction disqualify such a timepiece for use outside the bathtub (accidentally moving it in the wrong direction will indicate a longer dive time than actually available).

Or the 'Flieger' watches (pilot watches). Oh yes, here we need a pithy German label like 'Blitzkrieg'. It's the magic that counts, even if one has' to fight for a seat in the first rows of the 'sardine-class' to get closer to the cockpit.

Wristwatches with a stop function? Well, they are highly prized by collectors, usually represent the higher art of watchmaking, are expensive, and beautiful to look at, but ...

... seriously: If you need to measure time very accurately, it's no use if the watch can't do it properly. No, not from a technical point of view, but because the handling (especially when left on the wrist) becomes a fiddly job. There are many other things to be mentioned that make a *normal* stopwatch a serious instrument and not a toy on the wrist.

Before I forget: Those private engravings like 'To Dad from his children' or 'To my beloved husband John' – well, that reduces the value for a collector outside the family, unlike value-enhancing 'carvings' such as 'To Elvis from Priscilla' or 'VW 100,000 Kilometers'.

If we take a quick look at the larger ticking friends – the clocks – we find many nice and esthetic timepieces, but also, unfortunately, the French mantelpiece clocks, whose tastelessness is hard to beat. Once they had developed well-functioning table clocks, which were more than adequate for the needs of the time and which ran continuously and well for 8 days, the technical creativity disappeared somewhat and they came up with such dreadful products. They could well be used as emetics when people have adverse reactions against the standard products – 'look and throw up'.

Marble imitation housing and base with fire-gilded crap on top, such as scantily clad Greek goddesses surrounded by nude putti and between candlesticks on each side – brothel décor!

The prices on the market for this horological rubbish have dropped almost in free fall so that some of these watches might fly after you for free if you don't close the door on your way out of the store.

Looking back, I'm very glad I didn't pick up any of that stuff at auctions or elsewhere (well, yes – except for one or two) because a few years back you had to pay a lot of money for these dust-catchers.

But all of this is rather harmless and admittedly still a matter of opinion.

'An opinion is a judgment, viewpoint, or statement that is not conclusive, rather than facts, which are true statements' (Wiki).

Whatever, the following chapters leave no room for opinions; the madness, the irresponsibility, and the utter stupidity are facts – the sad truth about a cardinal derailment of the watchmaking industry.

And it can get worse

Now, all of this can be topped if, for example, someone comes up with the idea of permanently displaying the time in the dark with luminous paint containing radioactive substances as activators.

Besides the use for the military, there are of course other sensible applications in the professional field – but on a civilian wristwatch?

Well, the permanent glow of the old, luminous paint, activated by Radium (Radium 226), is only good in theory; in practice, it soon or later fades away completely, since the radium not only activates the luminous material (usually Zinc Sulfide) but also destroys it at the same time.

Let's sweep this under the carpet for now, but we'll look at it in more detail later.

Fortunately, such luminous paint has become quite harmless nowadays and is only a gimmick if you still 'must have it', or it can simply be ignored if the watch came with it.

It is a gimmick because, in the end, it is not such an ideal solution either (speaking of functionality).

Luminous paint of a newer type, Luminova, Superluminova, or similar, have at least removed the dangers of something that is more or less superfluous. But we no longer have the permanent glow of a radioactively activated luminous paint (working that way at least for some time), as we now always need frequent recharging.

True, these watches with modern luminous paint show the time in dark surroundings, but only if they had enough time to be recharged with light – strongly depending on the season, and use during the day. What you then see after some time in the dark can in most cases be described with one or two words: 'nothing' and 'almost nothing'.

If you have to leave the watch in the sun all day to poorly read the time for a short while at night, what's the practical use?

Honestly, how often have you tested this? Have you ever tried to read the time after midnight, even if the watch was exposed to sufficient light during the day? Have you ever looked at your wristwatch at night and seen something on a tiny dial without having to turn on the light?

If you want to know the time late at night without disturbing your spouse or others lying around, you use a readable bedside clock where you can illuminate the entire dial at the touch of a button.

Nevertheless, some watch owners often rave about how bright and clear they can see the hands and indices in the dark, but certainly not under normal circumstances or in a season with shorter daylight hours or bad weather conditions.

Timex has developed a luminous substance (Indiglo) that covers the whole of the dial and is charged at the touch of a button the current from the battery. But you can't do that with a purely mechanical watch; you need electricity.

With the advent of batteries in wristwatches, the luminous paint could also be replaced by bulbs that illuminate the entire dial or a digital display, or the 'juice' is used to light up LED numbers. An occasional look at the wristwatch at night is not too much of a drain on the battery.

And then, today, they even make luminous hands and numerals <u>in combination with the above</u> (!) – as if an evil fairy had whispered in the manufacturer's ear: *'Don't forget the luminous hands, or we'll kidnap your mother'*.

Have you ever noticed that most expensive luxury watch brands deliberately do without this stupid 'illumination'? Exceptions prove the rule also here (special watches or models). But when wealth is a prerequisite to buying such a watch, and wealth is furthermore based on intelligence (besides luck), then I have more sympathy than ever for the old Prussian electoral law, which only allowed rich people to vote.

Risks

So what are the main hazards when handling old watches that still have radioactive luminous paint on them?

If you simply wear such a watch and keep it closed, the dangers from the radioactive material can largely (but not always!!!) be ignored.

But as soon as the watch is opened, the stuff can be inhaled or ingested/swallowed (particles in the air or picked up with the finger, etc.) and once it has entered the body, it's highly carcinogenic.

Not only watchmakers open watches and thus put themselves at risk. Contemporaries who buy used vintage watches want to see pictures of the movement to assess what they are getting on the internet sales platform. Collectors also need to open watches to inspect the movement and verify the type and caliber.

Cleaning the case is best done with the movement removed. Some of the old, luminous paint, which has meanwhile fallen off and is possibly flying around inside for a long time, will come out in fine particles you might inhale or pick up with the fingers.

And if someone has overturned the little screw again that holds the winding stem with the crown in place, which you have to extract before taking out the movement, the angle lever on the other side falls off, and you have to remove the hands and the dial to fix it, putting you right into the middle of this radioactive filth.

But even without opening such a watch, there are (limited) dangers from radioactive radiation, especially the emission of Radon gas, which we will deal with later.

Whatever, the idea to be able to read the time in dark surroundings with the help of radioactively activated luminous paint, although gaslight or electric light were already used in normal households at that time (flashlights were also available), was the beginning or better the commercial continuation of an activity which, in this form, can only be regarded as a highly negligent, nitwitted derailment, at least from a certain state of science onwards.

The radioactive luminous paints have left behind radioactive waste for thousands – even millions – of years beyond the presumed end of our universe – which we now have to deal with.

In one particular case, the application of radioactive luminous paint on watches was associated with one of the worst chapters in modern working life, which must be described as highly reprehensible and a disgrace to humanity (see chapter 'The Radium Girls').

We give you Radium

Imagine some marketing freaks, bored watch producers, gaga dreamers, crackpot scientists, plus maybe an assistant horse-dropping collector, a ham-handed french-fry carver, and a few non-synchronous line-dancers; this could bring a crowd together, which could possibly – I say possibly – come up with such nonsense of radioactive activation of luminous material on civilian everyday watches.

But, alas, that's just not what happened.

What concerns the early beginnings, I had already accepted an excusing circumstance:

'For they did not – yet – know what they were doing'.

Radium in general (or rather the Radium isotope 226 when talking about watches, but we'll get to that later) was in the beginning generally considered to be beneficial to health; a cure for many things, a boon to mankind. In those days, there were products on the market such as Radium water, Radium soap, Radium toothpaste, Radium butter, Radium bread, Radium cosmetics, Radium cigarettes, and so on.

Spas lured customers with high levels of Radium in their environment and bathtubs; so why shouldn't some whackos try to make civilian watches 'glow' with that radioactive material? Perhaps they themselves had been exposed to the stuff for too long.

The Radium Girls

Let me briefly come to a story, which takes us to the lowest level of human behavior: It is about the 'Radium Girls'.

The 'Radium Girls' working in the U.S. Radium Corporation

When Archangel Gabriel will blow the final horn to announce Judgment Day, a very special bunch of people will be standing together awaiting just punishment – those involved in the scandal around the 'Radium Girls'.

Everyone passing by will be asked, 'are you one of them?'

If you can say 'no' or explain that you only have a mid-level criminal record for burglary and bank robbery, besides killing your mother for 15 dollars and 55 cents in her purse, you'll be politely asked to move on for now.

So, who exactly will be standing there?

Industry bosses, managers, shysters, paid scientists, bribed court people and corrupt politicians will be standing there together – all of them who were involved in this scandal.

Can it get any worse?

Many books have already been written about the poor 'Radium Girls', so just very briefly:

The 'Radium Girls' worked for the U.S. Radium Corporation (formerly Radium Luminous Material Corporation) and applied radioactive luminous paint to coat hands and dials. The paint was marketed under the name 'Undark'. They could have called the stuff 'Unintelligent' instead.

All this was done at their New Jersey plant. To get a fine tip on their brush, the girls frequently took it into their mouth and between their lips, ingesting the Radium-contaminated stuff. Having been told that this was absolutely harmless, some of them would even paint their fingernails or a tooth for the fun of it, to see them 'glow in the dark'.

At first, physical deterioration and general weakness could be observed. According to the medical 'wisdom' at this stage, with a lower life form − the shysters − playing for time, this wasn't recognized as something that would develop into fractures and necrosis of the jaws, anemia, and fragile bones.

In the negotiations with the employers about the working conditions and (later) about some compensation for the medical costs, the poor girls had to deal with these men, who will one day stand together as the bunch described above, while the $15.55-matricide will be waived through.

The Power of Radium at Your Disposal

Twenty-three years ago radium was unknown. Today, thanks to constant laboratory work, the power of this most unusual of elements is at your disposal. Through the medium of Undark, radium serves you safely and surely.

Does Undark really contain radium? Most assuredly. It is radium, combined in exactly the proper manner with zinc sulphide, which gives Undark its ability to shine *continuously* in the dark.

Manufacturers have been quick to recognize the value of Undark. They apply it to the dials of watches and clocks, to electric push buttons, to the buckles of bed room slippers, to house numbers, flashlights, compasses, gasoline gauges, autometers and many other articles which you frequently wish to see in the dark.

The next time you fumble for a lighting switch, bark your shins on furniture, wonder vainly what time it is *because of the dark*—remember Undark. *It shines in the dark.* Dealers can supply you with Undarked articles.

For interesting little folder telling of the production of radium and the uses of Undark address

To Manufacturers

The number of manufactured articles to which Undark will add increased usefulness is manifold. From a sales standpoint, it has many obvious advantages. We gladly answer inquiries from manufacturers and, when it seems advisable, will carry on experimental work for them. Undark may be applied either at your plant, or at our own.

The application of Undark is simple. It is furnished as a powder, which is mixed with an adhesive. The paste thus formed is painted on with a brush. It adheres firmly to any surface.

RADIUM LUMINOUS MATERIAL CORPORATION
58 PINE STREET • • • • NEW YORK CITY
Factories: Orange, N. J.   Mines: Colorado and Utah

UNDARK
Radium Luminous Material

Shines in the Dark

'UNDARK – 'most assuredly' containing Radium.

All the problems were at first blamed on the 'physical weakness' of these young girls who had been generously given the opportunity of light work, and now the employer cannot be held responsible when they already collapse under the weight of a decorating job with a brush in a pleasant working environment.

As things got worse and the horrible physical disfigurements became more and more visible, these bastards now blamed it on syphilis – yes, syphilis! What can you expect from such morally degenerated young girls?

The fact that all other employees of the company, male and female, in all other workplaces, did not suffer from physical weaknesses or such terrible deformities, didn't provoke any reaction other than the continuation of a condemnable legal trickery.

What's the difference between these lawyers and a bucket full of 'number two'? The bucket.

The fact that these poor girls repeatedly took a brush contaminated with radioactive paint into their mouths to sharpen it with their lips and ensure a fine line was perfidiously not recognized as a distinguishing feature from other activities in the house.

And then, unexpectedly, help came from a young American man: handsome, tall, athletic (U.S. Amateur Golf Champion), successful in his business, rich – every mother-in-law's dream and society's darling. Eben Byers – that was his name – showed the same symptoms as the girls after he had consumed 3 liters of Radium water a day on his doctor's orders to help heal a broken bone.

The connection to Radium became abundantly clear. The pressure was now coming from all sides. This was around the year 1930, but luminous paint containing Radium was still used in the watch industry until the late 1960s. Why, if you are not completely insane?

Well, how quickly can the winds of favor change! Even the Wall Street Journal has switched sides:

Not belonging to the regular daily papers and certainly not to the yellow press, their business is usually related to financial and economic issues. They repeat today's figures from different sources and try to tell you what will happen in the economy tomorrow, only to publish a clever article afterward about why it came the other way around.

'Mens sane in corpore sano' (this is Latin and means 'healthy mind in a healthy body') crawled up as a 'Leitmotif' and also showed how fast and deep one can fall again.

And when a flashy catch line comes to mind, one quickly forgets the fine manners. They now made fun of him after his death with the 'un-financial' headline: 'The Radium water worked fine until his jaw came off'.

He died badly deformed in 1932 and was buried in a lead-lined coffin. 33 years later, in 1965, his skeleton was exhumed to measure the Radium content in his bones.

Needless to say, the existence of Radium could have been confirmed without digging up a single gram of soil, simply by looking in the books. But they most likely wanted to see and hear their Geiger counters and the needle hammering against the end of the scale.

The decay of radioactive substances is measured in half-lives. Radium 226 has a half-life period of about 1,600 years, so basically everything still had to be there – like on an older watch when luminous paint with Radium as an activator was applied.

A half-life is the time it takes for 50% of the element to decay, then 50% of what's left, then 50% of the rest, and so on. The whole process is completed after 10 half-lives. 1,600 years = 50 % decay and 50% still left. 33 years (at the time of exhumation) = 1.03 % decay and 98.97 % left. The new elements on the next steps down the decay chain are also radioactive until everything has settled. We will go into more detail about half-lives and radioactive decay later in the book.

Just for completeness: The results after the exhumation were such that, of course, they confirmed the presence of Radium and the need for a lead-lining of the coffin, but a few hours in the fresh air, instead of looking at tables in the office – why not?

Finally, Dr. Arnold von Sochocky, one of the founders of the U.S. Radium Corporation (formerly the Radium Luminous Material Corporation) and developer of the 'Undark' also fell ill with the same symptoms. He was, however, able to help the poor girls, especially as everything became even more obvious. Unfortunately, this was not the case for the watch industry, which continued to play around with this toxic material for decades to come.

Dr. Sochocky is often credited with the invention of radium-based luminous paint, but this isn't entirely correct – although he was involved in this area very early on.

The dam broke, and the girls received at least some financial compensation – but they did not recover their health, and many lost their lives.

Dr. Sochocky died in terrible circumstances at the age of 45.

On the contrary, his laboratory assistant Florence E. Wall, reached the age of 95.

So much for comments about women only being allowed to make coffee and look pretty in their workplaces. It can have its advantages not to be involved too much in the actual work process ...

Seriously again, there were other reasons:

According to Florence Wall's recollections, the chemists had protective equipment in the workplace, unlike the girls who applied the radioactive luminous paint, and who were also told to always sharpen the brush with their lips – that would be the best (and cheapest) way to do it.

How to implement such an insanity

Reading the time in the dark has become a 'must' even in the civilian sector, but it's a silly thing on a normal wristwatch, especially when leaving radioactive waste behind for millions of years (Radium 226 is not the worst in this respect!)

The use of today's luminous paint on watches is admittedly a good step from 'dangerous' to 'harmless' but nevertheless rather useless, as things rarely work in an ideal way, as already described. Perhaps a bit harshly put, but certainly not entirely wrong.

As far as the old, radioactive luminous paints are concerned, it must be said clearly: Basic chemistry and physics, and especially the consequences of any activity in these fields, should be understood by scientists dealing with radioactive substances before they get started. But you can never be sure, or they just didn't care. If the beginnings of the nonsense are still halfway excusable, the behavior of the main protagonists should have gradually adapted to scientific progress. Today, one would have to demand such intelligence from a nightcrawler (at both ends).

However, 'representation of interest' is not too seldom a special law of nature for some scientists. For the right amount of money, you might get a confirmation from professor 'Bribed' that gravity really does pull up, not down, and that only air pressure above 850 hPa keeps everything on the ground.

For the old luminous paint, you basically needed three things:

1. **A luminescent substance:** A suitable substance has been found in the form of Zinc Sulfide. It appears in nature and can also be artificially produced.
2. **An activator**. Activation can be induced by various things, whereby the luminescent substance can react to more of them and differently; but we want a permanent glow.
3. **A binding agent:** A lacquer that holds everything together and keeps things stuck on the surface.

Points 1. and 3. are simple. But if you want to have a permanent activator independent of light, it must be radioactive and therefore always dangerous.

Why Radium?

When we speak of luminescent substances and their ability to glow (without heat like the glowing iron of a blacksmith) after being charged in whatever way, we distinguish according to the duration of the emitted light: <u>fluorescent</u>, with a very short duration of less than 1/1000 of a second when the excitation source is removed, and <u>phosphorescent</u> (capable of storing), with a duration equal to or greater than 1/1000 of a second, up to minutes and hours.

Excitation can occur (among other things) through chemical reactions, exposure to daylight or UV light, or electrical energy. We also have bioluminescence (organic reaction) which we, for instance, know from the 'headlight elater', a species of the click beetle (Pyrophorus noctilucus), or some fungi like the luminescent panellus (Panellus stipticus).

The poisonous toadstool doesn't glow but is occasionally used as an intoxicant by some weird individuals, preferring natural dope to the stuff in the disco. Perhaps some of the 'specialists' of the watchmaking industry had picked the wrong mushrooms?

All but one of the activators have a fading effect, so the luminous substance must always be 'reloaded'.

There is only that one type of activator that is permanently active – yes, you know it: a radioactive substance (initially Radium 226). It causes a permanently activated glow, but over time, it also destroys the structure of the activated material itself, so that sooner or later the glow will disappear. But at the same time, it ensures that the dangers of radioactivity will remain as radioactive waste (inactive glow, but continued radioactivity) for thousands and thousands of years – the effect is gone, but the damage remains, in the case of Samarium 147 the half-life is 106 billion years = over 1 trillion years before everything is gone!

But then we often hear a sentence with two errors: 'The Radium on my watch has disappeared, it no longer glows.'

Error No. 1: The Radium itself doesn't glow. It has only weak properties in this regard and, as I said, serves only as an activator.

Error No. 2: The Radium isn't gone either – it's still there, almost completely, together with the derived products of the decay chain.

The 'secret' of radioactivity

'Simply' put again: Radioactivity is the spontaneous act of emitting ionizing radiation by unstable variants of atomic nuclei (isotopes or nuclides). They decay by emitting alpha, beta, and gamma radiation and strive for stability by 'flinging' particles away until they reach a stable state. They do this until the final stage in a decay chain, thus always forming other atomic nuclei.

The two terms isotope and nuclide (the latter introduced later) basically mean the same thing. There are numerous explanations for why we have two terms, what the difference is, and when to use one or the other. For a general understanding of the matter, you can just say 'one of the two is redundant'; otherwise it depends on context and usage, and is often confused by the scientists themselves. Some 'hair-splitters' saw an urgent need for a distinction, but this usually comes from 'scholars' who have nothing else to offer in terms of real 'discoveries'. We therefore simply call them, quite neutrally, 'variant'.

Since this is not a scientific book, but rather an 'analysis' of a 'cardinal derailment' of the watchmaking industry, we shall only briefly touch on a few key points.

Our elements consist of atoms, a nucleus and a shell, and their own little world inside and around – protons, neutrons, electrons, which in turn consist of even smaller particles like up-quarks, down-quarks, orbitons, spinons, holons.

And there are photons (quanta) that have no mass. They come along with highly penetrating gamma radiation. Since they have no mass, there is hardly any interaction with other matter; they practically pass through concrete walls and can be stopped only by thick and massive lead shielding. The man who walks through the wall – the dream of many a scientist how to enter the office.

Other things have been discovered over time, like the antiparticles – anti-electron (positron), anti-neutron with their own anti-up-quarks and anti-down-quarks, etc., etc.

The atoms of various elements differ by the number of protons they have. But we don't have *the* Copper atom or *the* Gold atom or *the* Radium atom as such. Our naturally occurring elements usually consist of several (stable) atoms with the same amount of protons, which in turn differ by their number of neutrons and are combined in a certain mixture.

Besides those, we also have the unstable atoms of some elements. They don't like their instability and try to reach a stable state by 'throwing away' protons (+charge) together with neutrons (neutral charge), electrons (- charge), or positrons (+charge) – that's what we call radioactivity.

There can also be an exchange of protons and neutrons.

This goes on until a stable state is reached, often beyond the end of the days of our planet.

Unbelievable what these nutty guys have put on the hands and dials of watches!

If you can still follow: This process is divided into alpha decay, beta plus decay, beta minus decay, and the specific radioactive radiation associated with each. We also see the highly penetrating gamma radiation, which is another thing that occurs along with alpha- and beta decay when there is enough energy left, and occasionally also X-rays, resulting from a sudden deceleration or acceleration of charged particles.

It all started with the 'Big Bang' when matter was created in different forms. The theory says, that at the same time also anti-matter came along, which should have been of an equal amount. An equal amount of nothing (anti-matter) for every something (matter). In our atomic world, these would be proton and anti-proton, neutron and anti-neutron, electron and anti-electron (also known as positron) – anti-particles, the real existence of Nothing.

And there is more to the theory: Matter and anti-matter annihilate each other whenever they meet, which should have been the case immediately after the Big Bang – leaving back nothing, no matter, and no anti-matter.

Well … in this case the newly created universe should have collapsed immediately. But we still have matter around us, otherwise, nothing would exist.

They now suspect, that there has been 'a little surplus' on the side of the matter (due to an 'asymmetry violation of physical laws'), leaving today's matter around us. In other words, all anti-matter has annihilated itself together with the corresponding amount of matter, leaving just a surplus of matter.

Symmetry in thinking versus 'asymmetry violation' in physical laws should lead to the conclusion, that there is no more anti-matter left, otherwise it would annihilate more matter.

Right?

Yet scientists are desperately searching for antimatter.

What?

If their own theory says that there was just a surplus of matter left, as any remaining anti-matter would otherwise have destroyed more matter, what are they looking for?

You might think it doesn't matter. Whatever, as long as they are looking for nothing, it's a lot better than playing around with radioactive luminous paint …

Back to the Radium. The watch no longer 'glows' at night – what a pity! It can only cause cancer …

How can anyone, not totally insane, produce and apply such a dangerous nonsense?

The process of decay can be a single step towards stability, or several steps down a long ladder (sometimes even a step up in between, depending on the change in the number of protons).

As I have mentioned before, the ugly stuff Radium 226 in the luminous paint on our watch has a half-life of 1,600 years. That means that it takes 1,600 years to decay to half (50%) or 160 years to lose 5%.

More bad news: The rest hasn't gone up in smoke; it's still there in the form of other radioactive substances, often more dangerous than Radium 226 itself. Here, the remaining time for the next elements in the decay chain, before a stable state is reached, is very short, but when it comes to other idiotically used substances, they may, in certain cases, be around beyond the existence of our universe.

'Oh, I've discovered something wonderful, I can make my watch glow and read the time in the dark.'

It would make me very happy if we could put all this down to the 'inzested' intelligence of Little Joe Hickerberg.

Now let's look at the decay chain containing Radium 226 (opposite page).

You can see that it starts with Uranium 238 and goes all the way down to Lead 206, and somewhere in between you'll find the radioactive element mixed into the fluorescent paint – *our* starting point Radium 226. I have highlighted this in grey for easier reference.

There are half-lives in the decay table between 0.00016 seconds and 4.5 billion years. One particular element (Polonium 214) has this half-life of 0.00016 seconds, and if you count 10 half-lives, it's only around for 0.0016 seconds before it's gone forever. Don't ask me how they measure that.

Once the decay process has started, you will soon find all decay products in a certain amount on a watch with such radioactive luminous paint; it is just a question of different residence time until a total half is gone and the next half of the remaining amount and so on. The continuing steps come immediately. Soon all the radioactive decay products are represented (save the ones which have meanwhile totally disappeared – in the case of the Radium 226 after 16,000 years = 10 half-lives).

DEYAY CHAIN OF URANIUM 238 TO LEAD 236

Element	Decay	Half-life	Deyas to
Uranium 238	α, γ	4,5 billion years	Thorium 234
Thorium 234	β, γ	24 days	Protactinium 234
Protactinium 234	β, γ	6,7 hours (234 Pa) 1,2 minutes (234 mPa)	Uranium 234
Uranium 234	α, γ	245,000 years	Thorium 230
Thorium 230	α, γ	75,000 years	Radium 226
Radium 226	α, γ	1,600 years	Radon 222
Radon 222	α	3,8 days	Polonium 218
Polonium 218	α	3,1 minutes	Lead 214 (99,98 %)
	β	3,1 minutes	Astatine 218 (0,02 %)
Lead 214	β, γ	26,8 minutes	Bismuth 214
Astatine 218	α	1,5 seconds	Bismuth 214
Bismuth 214	α	19,9 minutes	Polonium 214 (99,98 %)
	β	19,9 minutes	Thallium 210 (0,02 %)
Polonium 214		0,00016 seconds	Lead 210
Thallium 210		1,3 minutes	Lead 210
Lead 210	β, γ	22,3 years	Bismuth 210
Bismuth 210	β	5 days	Polonium 210 (99,99987 %)
	α	5 days	Thallium 206 (0,00013 %)
Polonium 210	α, γ	138 days	Lead 206
Thallium 206	β	4 minutes	Lead 206
Lead 206		**STABLE**	**BINGO!**

α = alpha, β = beta, γ = gamma

What was also used besides Radium?

Radium 226

The common radioactive activator was initially Radium (Radium 266). In the civilian sector, it is found mainly around WW I, until the late 1960s with highlights in the late 1930s to the 1950s, when the paint applied on the dial and hands (also subsequently replaced or intensified) became thicker and thicker without regard to aesthetics.

We have looked at Radium 226 in its decay chain and with its half-life. Have there been any other 'ideas' in this regard?

Yes, you can bet on it, stupidity knows no bounds!

Strontium 90

Let's start with the 'bone seeker', as another radioactive stuff is called, officially known as Strontium 90 and also an activator for luminous paint on watches from 1950 onwards. It was rarely used because such watches were only produced for a relatively short time.

The wearers of those watches didn't really feel 'comfortable' on the wrist, and this nonsense was soon abandoned.

Strontium 90 has only a short half-life of 28.8 years and 'seeks' the wrist bones of the watch wearer (from the outside through the watch!). It, however, can remain in the body much longer, up to 50 years – in the bones, bone marrow, or teeth – causing bone cancer, cancer of adjacent tissue, and leukemia.

Strontium has a similar structure to Calcium, which is essential for our teeth and bones, and when it comes along, the body mistakenly deposits it in the bones. When God created man, *He* also gave us bones and teeth that need Calcium, but would *He* have thought that some morons would put Strontium on our wrists?

Strontium 90 is already all around us as a product of nuclear fission (nuclear fallout). It can be found in the teeth of people born after 1963 as a result of atomic bomb testing.

Together with Iodine 131 and Cesium 134, Strontium 90 was one of the most harmful isotopes that affected human health after the Chernobyl disaster.

Strontium 90 decays via Yttrium 90 into the stable Zirconium 90.

Element	Decay	Half-life	Decays to
Strontium 90	β -	28,8 years	Yttrium 90
Yttrium 90	β -	64 hours	Zirconium 90
Zirconium 90		**STABLE**	

β - = beta minus

'Oh, I've discovered something wonderful, I can make my watch glow and read the time in the dark.'

Samarium 147 after Promethium 147

Take a deep breath – the worst is yet to come: Promethium 147 and especially the following element in the decay chain, Strontium 147.

Do you occasionally enjoy a glass or two? Then by all means do it now; I hope you have something strong to drink at hand. Perhaps you can find some weed to smoke, or at least take your 'all is lost anyway' attitude, because what I am about to tell you now will be beyond your wildest dreams and will further weaken your faith in humanity.

Can our species really be that stupid?

I was tempted to say that only a unicellular organism could be so senseless as to do such a thing, but in the spirit of 'political correctness', you have to be careful in all directions these days, including bacteria, protists, and yeast.

No, multicellular human beings have done that:

Someone, obviously not in his right mind, had the idea to replace Radium 226 or Strontium 90 with Promethium 147 as an activator for luminescent substances.

We might think that this development was just the result of a bunch of mad scientists being locked up in an asylum, and the doctors were looking for something to occupy them. Why not experiment with luminous paint for watches? But how, in such a case, could anything get out and into the watchmaking industry?

But let's take it one step at a time.

There was one very last element that man had not yet found. Everything was there except the one with 61 protons – a gap in the periodic table.

Scientists had already created some elements artificially and added them to the periodic table, but the natural element with 61 protons remained mysterious and untraceable.

And then came the atomic bombs, putting an end to a nightmare. Perhaps Ricefield-Marshal Gaga Nippomoto had dipped his writing brush into his sake cup too often before sharpening it with his lips; otherwise, how could he have thought they would get away with what they had started?

During the preceding research on the atomic bomb and experiments with Uranium, the missing element with 61 protons suddenly stuck its head out as a fission product.

Some scientists had previously claimed to have found this element with 61 protons. Two Italians from Florence, already called it 'Florentinum' – based on a misinterpretation of their observations. Two scientists from the University of Illinois called their discovery 'Illinium', but none of this could be confirmed.

It was not until 1945 that it was discovered at Oak Ridge National Laboratory (ORNL), Tennessee.

Jacob A. Marinsky, Lawrence E. Glendenin, and Charles D. Coryell had finally discovered it as the said fission product of Uranium. Because of the need for secrecy in connection with military research during the Second World War, this wasn't published until 1947.

So, do we have this particular element Promethium, as it was later called, on the watches (Promethium 127), that might never have been found otherwise, as a consequence of Pearl Harbor? 'Made in Japan' in a wider sense?

To be fair, it should be mentioned in this connection that it was a Japanese company called Nemote & Co. Ltd. that later developed the harmless, non-radioactive luminous paint for watches, known as LumiNova, which was used from 1968, although the Swiss had already produced something similar called 'SuperLite' before the Japanese.

Initially, a joint venture was founded ('LumiNova Switzerland'), with raw material from Japan, which was refined in Switzerland.

Eventually, the Swiss company RC Tritec AG (Ltd.) did it all on their own under license in Switzerland, and later came out with the 'Superluminova' that is widely used today.

Back to Promethium: The scientists were scared and had realized what they do by developping an atomic bomb. Nobody, therefore, wanted to have his name connected to this finally discovered element with 61 protons.

Grace Mary Coryell, Charles Coryell's wife, came up with the idea of calling it Promethium, after the Greek titan Prometheus. He had brought fire to mankind, and because this was not only a blessing but also responsible for terrible destruction, he was banished by the Greek gods.

So, really – you find the last unknown element on this planet and the wife at home picks the name for it and lets the 'connoisseur of ancient Greek history' hang out.

But this was meant to be more a warning to everyone – except a few madmen in the watch industry (at least the part that tinkered with the radioactive luminous paint at that time).

Promethium 147 on the watch was even loudly advertised. A large watch company ranted enthusiastically and mentally totally absent:

'The XYZ-Model is for men who work hard and demand a lot. Waterproof, dustproof, anti-magnetic... with a strong luminous dial, but without gamma radiation. The luminous paint with promethium is not dangerous ...'

An absurdity, a nonsense, a sign of ignorance – too hard to believe!

Promethium has a half-life of only 2.6 years and will soon be gone, but that's not the absurdity I'm talking about.

And yes, on the face of it, this silly advertising slogan of ignorant people isn't entirely wrong (if the watch was also reliably waterproof or antimagnetic, I don't know, but it doesn't really matter).

There is indeed no gamma radiation here, which only occurs when there is enough energy left over in an alpha or beta decay (beta minus in this case).

But ... Promethium 147 does not stay Promethium 147 and it's part of a decay chain like all radioactive elements, and the next stage is coming very soon in this case and it won't be only a short intermediate step.

After Promethium 147 comes Samarium 147 with a half-life of – hold on tight – 106 billion years (!!!) before it reaches the final, stable stage of Neodymium 143.

106 billion years before half is gone, 1.06 trillion years until it's all gone until all the radioactive stuff on such a watch has decayed.

This is hazardous waste staying beyond the existence of our universe, and the universe of our universe ...

And then, they advertise and blather about Promethium 147 on the watch with a minuscule half-life of only 2.6 years, which very soon decays to Samarium 147 for all eternity (actually, the process begins immediately).

Ouch! Luke 23:34: *'Lord forgive them, for they do not know what they do!*

Admittedly, Samarium 147 also has no gamma radiation along with its radioactive and aggressive alpha radiation. However, it is highly toxic, a serious fire hazard, and even explosive.

Of course, we only have small amounts of the latter here. But once inside the body, it's just as dangerous as all alpha emitters – otherwise, it stays around us for ten times 106 billion years (!!!) – a dimension close to that of this idiocy.

Element	Decay	Half-life	Decays to
Promethium 147	β -	2,6 years	Samarium 147
Samarium 147	α	106 billion years	Neodymium 143
Neodymium 143		STABLE	

β - = beta minus, α = alpha

'Oh, I've discovered something wonderful, I can make my watch glow and read the time in the dark.'

I think the ancient Egyptians would not have put sticks in the sand to tell the time by the shadows they cast, and Galileo Galilei would have preferred to go for a walk rather than discover the laws of the pendulum if they had known where all this was leading to.

And I don't even think of the French mantel clocks ...

In case you're interested: You can find the description 'Pm' as a hint to Promethium on the dial (which is of course long gone and has become Samarium 147 – forever).

Tritium

Tritium as an activator later replaced Radium 226 and other radioactive rubbish from the 1960s to the 1990s. At first, it was thought to be more or less harmless, but today we know better.

Tritium still exists in the form of GTLS – Gaseous Tritium Light Source. Everything is now put together with the luminous substance in small, sealed tubes. It's basically safe, but in case of breakage, there is a risk that Tritium, being a gas, will enter our body more easily and quickly.

This Tritium light is used not only for watches (very small tubes) but also for emergency lights or key rings.

It can also be found in special telescopic sights.

Tritium has a half-life of only 12.3 years. It was often used only very sparingly (mixed into the luminous paint), considering its price compared to the value of the newer watches, which were becoming ever cheaper in the market for affordable timepieces.

Initially used in a bonded but open form, Tritium has recently come back into focus as a special source of danger, more so than in the past when it was thought to be the solution to the problem (or at least reducing the dangers) – another mistake they had made.

Tritium is a gas. It can escape from the luminous paint. Its radiation can only reach three to four millimeters into the air, but you are wearing your watch not over your wrist, but on your wrist. And here, Tritium can enter the body through plastic cases (often used for watches of cheaper type) and then through the skin (and, of course, by inhalation).

The University of Innsbruck, Austria carried out a test with 108 students. Those who wore such a plastic watch with a luminous substance activated by Tritium had a ten times higher concentration of Tritium in their urine than a comparison group without such junk on their wrist.

Do you want to have your urine tested frequently if you carry this radioactive crap around in a plastic vintage watch?

A Franco-Belgian study (2008) concluded that the radiological effects of Tritium have so far been underestimated.

Human DNA may be affected and problems may occur, especially during pregnancy.

The biological activity of Tritium is also of particular concern. Like Hydrogen, it can enter the material cycle and, as a radioactive component, damage drinking water.

Element	Decay	Half-life	Decays to
Tritium	ß -	12,3 years	Helium
Helium		STABLE	

ß - = beta minus

'Oh, I've discovered something wonderful, I can make my watch glow and read the time in the dark.'

The main danger from watches containing radioactive paint does not come primarily from external radiation effects (although that is also possible in certain constellations) but from inhalation or ingestion of loose particles.

This can happen whenever the watch is opened by collectors, or during a service at the watchmaker's workplace when the watch is disassembled (and a normal service requires complete disassembly and cleaning, not just a little oiling here and there).

Hence, particles can be inhaled and enter the respiratory tract or – picked up with the fingers – enter the body via the esophagus, perhaps with the next pizza.

The dangers, which emanate from Radon (Radon 222), causing severe problems in connection with this radioactive luminous paint on watches, are dealt with in the next chapter (no, not Radium, Radon, a gas, and the next decay product after Radium 226).

In the beginning, the health problems caused by radioactivity were not immediately recognized; people just didn't know any better.

For years, they were still running around on the radioactively contaminated nuclear test sites, after everything had cooled down, with the most serious consequences resulting from this radiation exposure.

It took some time before such dangers became increasingly apparent – at least to most people – with a remarkable delay in the civilian watch industry, deliriously happy on their new playground.

These old (vintage) watches are still around, being collected, bought and sold, given away, and taken apart, not only by watchmakers but also by collectors.

But even unopened they can be a serious hazard, not to mention all the old bedside- and desk clocks, lying around or standing everywhere, as 'heirlooms' that you should dispose of but don't want to.

Beware of radioactive waste!

If the radioactive stuff gets into the body (inhaled or ingested) or if it has penetrated from the outside due to radioactive radiation, cancer is the main consequence if something goes wrong.

But that's not all!

When exposed to this radioactive material, *one also participates in a macabre lottery.*

We know two categories of health risks resulting from this useless and highly negligent idea of putting radioactive elements on consumer goods, such as watches, to activate luminous substances.

Deterministic damage: The word says it all. The amount, the dose, the time of exposure, and the distance, determine the damage. A little of it – little damage, a lot of it – a lot of damage.

In this case, we are talking about cell damage. The severity automatically increases with the dose, up to a fatal outcome.

Stochastic damage: Stochastic means 'lottery'. Any amount can cause damage, no matter how small, and a large amount of exposure can remain harmless, no matter how large. Like the other way around in the lottery, you can 'win' with a small stake and get nothing with a large stake.

If one is affected, we do not have a cell damage, but a cell modification.

And the worst of it: You do not know immediately whether you have 'won' or 'lost' because you have to wait for the next generation to see the result.

The cells remain intact, no problem for your own body, but the DNA is changed and passed on to the next generation as a genetic defect.

The phenomenon of stochastic damage is nowadays more and more intensively dealt with when looking at such hazards.

'Oh, I've discovered something wonderful, I can make my watch glow and read the time in the dark.'

Radon Gas (Radon 222)

We have seen that in the decay chain from Uranium 238 to Lead 206, where we also find Radium 226, Radon 222 is the next step after Radium 226.

It is also highly dangerous, and moreover, it's a gas that easily gets outside, and, of course, it is inhaled a lot faster than solid particles.

Radon 222 is not only a problem when it comes to watches with luminous paint containing Radium.

It is all around us and gets into the house and other places. When it accumulates and is not dispersed by ventilation, it poses a danger and is the second leading cause of lung cancer after smoking.

Radon gas not only enters enclosed spaces when Uranium decays in soil and rock, but we can also bring it into the home through a variety of sources:

A collection of aeronautical instruments, photographic lenses (coating) from a certain period, some ceramics produced until 1970, cloisonné jewelry and vases, granite plates in the kitchen or elsewhere, concrete products, and ... in the 'glow-in-the-dark' watches and clocks with radioactive luminescent paint.

The UNESCO has initiated and supported studies on the potential hazards in private households arising from Radon 222. Several universities around the world participated and contributed their results, including the Northampton University in Northampton and the Kingston University.

No, this Kingston University is not located in a sunny place in the Caribbean, but in London. They do have something like a college in Jamaica's capital — a public Christian secondary school — but, the 'radio activities' on the island consist mainly of reggae music, inundating the listeners day in and day out with an almost uninterrupted high frequency.

These two English universities focused on the dangers of Radon associated with collecting and handling vintage (military) watches containing Radium.

For this purpose, they studied 30 old watches of this type, consisting of British, Swiss, and American timepieces, and pointed out that millions of these watches are still in circulation.

The findings were frightening and confirmed a serious health hazard for collectors and their families, with smokers being particularly at risk (additional exposure).

All watches together had a dangerous Radon concentration 67 times (!) above the national maximum of 200 becquerels per cubic meter (Bq/m3) and more than 130 times (!!!) above the national target (!!!).

In particular, three watches in poor condition showed values of special concern.

If you have a further interest in this topic, search the Internet by using the keywords 'Kingston University' or 'University of Northampton' in conjunction with the word 'Radon'.

'Oh, I've discovered something wonderful, I can make my watch glow and read the time in the dark.'

Heidi, Heidi ...

Heidi, Heidi, your world are the mountains,
Heidi, Heidi, because up here you are at home.

Yes, now we come to Switzerland, the first and actually only country, if you take the strictness and seriousness of action as a yardstick, that consequently deals with the remains of this derailment with radioactive luminous paint on watches.

In summary, one can say: 'Let's get rid of this garbage!'

Switzerland is still the most important watch country with a large share of global sales. China leads only by the number of watches sold, but many of them are mere junk and 'tick' in the lowest price category.

Funny: the best customers for the expensive Swiss watches are the Chinese themselves, but you don't have to eat what you cook ...

Whatever, since April 2018, anyone who deals with such watches – be it ownership, collecting, repairing, private buying and selling, professional trading, exhibiting, etc. needs a special license.

Such a license can only be granted upon application, but only after attending an official seminar on radiation protection and related fields (also private individuals).

Moreover, you also have to prove that there is enough 'grease on the chain' (money available) to get rid of the stuff if it becomes necessary, also in the future.

In addition, internal regulations have to be set up (in case of a business activity) and adequate documentation regarding the inventory has to be kept and provided.

When passing on the watch(es), even as a gift, one must make sure that the next person in Switzerland meets these requirements with his own license. An urgent warning is given not to simply throw everything in the trash can, pointing out serious consequences in this case.

The option is left open to have any radioactive material removed from the dial and hands by a professional and licensed company and replaced with non-radioactive luminous paint, especially if someone wants to hold on to a family heirloom or military souvenir. This, however, might create a problem that is often observed when dealing with watch collectors.

For some of these guys, such a replacement is a blasphemy, a sacrilege, a disfigurement of the collection piece. I can only hope that someone won't cross my way with his beloved vintage car, not willing to replace wearing parts on brakes, steering, or the like.

The Swiss action Plan 'Radium':

Switzerland also wants to eliminate this problem regarding the old production sites. For this purpose, they have combed the whole country (which is not so small when you unfold the mountains on a map).

So far, they have found 80% of the former sites where radioactive paint was applied on watches, and 20% of these localities still pose a danger to the public.

In Switzerland, it was common early on for the watch industry to give work over the winter time to farmers and people dependent on the seasons. Identifying all these former 'private enterprises' will probably never be possible, as so much has changed over time.

Some environmentally conscious Swiss individuals have unleashed a spicy vocabulary in response. It ranges from bitter mockery and malice about this irresponsible stupidity, to sharp condemnation of those who should have known better over time. Occasionally, the ideas are almost reminiscent of the fate of Oliver Cromwell*.

* For the ones not so familiar with good old English traditions: Oliver Cromwell, Lord Protector of England, Scotland, and Ireland, was exhumed in 1661 and posthumously hanged. His head was then placed for some years on a 20-foot stick above Westminster Hall.

Oh my God, this can really make you angry!

The Basel Watch Fair recently introduced a new concept, a continued development from a classical fair to a platform for sensory experiences. How about putting some exhumed skulls of radium nuts at the main entrance?

Elsewhere: Some watchmakers principally refuse to work on such watches. A large and renowned watch manufacturer f. i. had officially declared that they would no longer work (maintenance/repair) on watches of unknown origin containing radioactive luminous paint, leaving only a small gap in the door for their own products from that period.

The nightmare is over

With the introduction of Luminova and Superluminova (among other in-house products of some watch companies), the danger of radioactive materials in luminous paints has been eliminated – but not the danger of this waste applied on older watches, which will continue to be around us, in some case beyond the existence of our universe.

In many places, spare parts such as contaminated hands and dials are still lying around. Collectors often find dried radioactive luminous paint in the old vials.

As far as these old watches are concerned, things are unfortunately the way they are.

And the watches of today? Do we really need this particular way of illuminating the dial and the hands?

I have already mentioned the rather dubious value of new and harmless luminous paint on wristwatches, but this book is mainly about the dangers arising from the old radioactive luminous paints.

So, coming to the end:

What has been applied?

I don't want to go into too much detail about how to find out exactly what you have on the hands and dial of an old watch, lumed in this stupid fashion, this would be too far leading. Sometimes you find 'Ra' (for Radium) or other designations marked on the dial, but the paint may have been completely or partially renewed (with whatever type) or applied in thicker layers afterward.

Collectors have all the time in the world to play around with their watches, watchmakers have to use their time more efficiently – better no work on this crap at all! Otherwise, an appropriate Geiger counter (not the trash you often find on the market) will show alpha-, beta- and gamma radiation. A Radon test confirms Radium (the only substance with radon in the decay chain).

Several light tests (preferably with UV light) will sometimes quickly show what you have. The Zinc Sulfide also reacts to light. If there is no or hardly any reaction, we usually have Radium and an almost completely destroyed luminous material, although the latter may briefly react at the 'last minute'.

If there is a stronger reaction (even after short exposure to UV light), we have a remnant of Tritium (half-life 12.3 years) with the Zinc Sulfide still halfway intact. The Zinc Sulfide reacts even better to light than the new Luminova material (alkaline earth aluminate), but the glow fades very quickly, so it cannot be used without constant recharging, unlike the new materials which can keep the effect somewhat longer.

Do not look for Promethium 147 (when you see 'Pm' on the dial). Enthusiastically advertised as a new 'wonder material', it has disappeared after a very short time and decayed into the not advertised or not even mentioned radioactive Samarium 147 and remains there – for ten times 106 billion (!) years.

**Two watches with radioactive luminous paint (Radium).
The original white dial on the second one has darkened due
to Radium burn and the paint has partially crumbled off.**

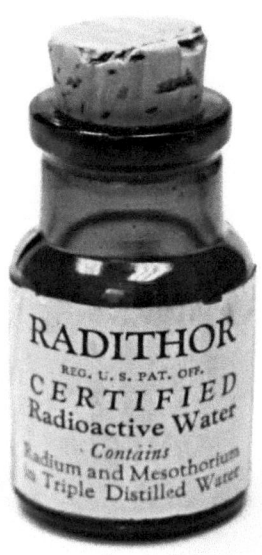

RADITHOR: The remedy that also sealed the fate of Eben Byers (see chapter 'The Radium Girls'). In the three times (!!!) distilled water, Radium 226 (the stuff on the watches), Radium 228 (a sister isotope), and Mesothorium I, were dissolved, resulting in an activity of one microcurie (old unit of measurement). The 'remedy' was produced in 1931 by Bailey Radium Laboratories, New Jersey, USA, and was touted as a 'cure for the living dead' and 'eternal sunshine', with healing properties for numerous diseases and miraculously replenishing the human organism from within through ionic radiation. Doctors who distributed it among their patients received a 17% discount. Because of the high price, it had been mainly rich people who took it. In the case of Eben Byers, the doctor was able to prescribe three liters a day – a dose that was several times lethal. This stuff did not have to be officially withdrawn from the market. Due to critical press reports, the company did so voluntarily.

Cheap Radium water from the economy barrel for the poorer contemporaries. Since – as in many other alleged radium products – little or no Radium was put in because of the high cost, most people escaped unscathed.

Furniture polish containing Radium.

Can of soap containing Radium.

Oven polish containing Radium. 'Shines brightest, lasts longest.'

Butter containing Radium.

Radium horror in eighteen eerie chapters of a silent film series from 1919. You don't have to be strangled by the 'rubber man'. Buying a vintage wristwatch or clock might do the trick. Some people still like to open their treasured radium-contaminated timepieces and fiddle around with them, on the workbench or the kitchen table.